**Anchor** THE NEW ANCHOR BOOK OF

Freestyle

EMBROIDERY STITCHES

Anchor

THE NEW ANCHOR BOOK OF

Freestyle

EMBROIDERY STITCHES

D&C

David and Charles

About the Embroidery Designer

The designs in this book were created by Joan Gordon, an embroiderer who has contributed to magazines including *Popular Crafts* and *Sewing World*. She has also demonstrated at craft shows and has presented craft on TV for Gutermann.

A DAVID & CHARLES BOOK

David & Charles is a subsidiary of F + W (UK) Ltd., an F + W Publications Inc. company

Published in association with
COATS CRAFTS UK

First published in the UK in 1987
Revised edition published 1997
This edition published 2005

Distributed in North America
by F + W Publications, Inc.
4700 East Galbraith Road
Cincinnati, OH 45236
1-800-289-0963

A catalogue record for this book is available from the British Library.

ISBN 0 7153 1917 5

Embroidery designs and project makes by Joan Gordon
Photography by Karl Adamson, Kim Sayer and Julien Busselle
Text originally compiled by Eve Harlow and revised for this edition by Betsy Hosegood

Printed in Singapore by KHL Printing Co Pte Ltd.
for David & Charles
Brunel House   Newton Abbot   Devon

Executive Editor   Cheryl Brown
Desk Editor   Ame Verso
Project Editor   Betsy Hosegood
Art Editor   Prudence Rogers
Designer   Sarah Underhill
Production Controller   Ros Napper

Visit our website at www.davidandcharles.co.uk

David & Charles books are available from all good bookshops; alternatively you can contact our Orderline on (0)1626 334555 or write to us at FREEPOST EX2 110, David & Charles Direct, Newton Abbot, TQ12 4ZZ (no stamp required UK mainland).

Contents

Introduction	6
Materials and Equipment	7
Transferring a Design	10
Using a Hoop or Frame	12
Working the Embroidery	14
Embroidery Ideas	16
Framing Your Work	22
Freestyle Stitches	24
Suppliers	64
Index	64

Introduction

Freestyle embroidery covers most of the embroidery stitches you are likely to have picked up along life's path and many you haven't yet learned. These stitches can be worked on almost any fabric from linen to velvet and can be used to create pictures or to embellish clothes, accessories and soft furnishings.

With freestyle embroidery you have the capacity to create more texture and variety of line than even the most adventurous painter or textile designer. You can layer stitch over stitch and colour over colour to create brilliant tapestries or work with limited stitches and hues to produce pieces of great style and elegance. With such variety of design sources available today and so many stitches at your disposal there really are no limits.

Variety of Stitches

Over the thousands of years that people have been decorating clothes and artefacts, countless stitches have been invented and reinvented. The Chinese are thought to have been embroidering garments as long ago as 3,000BC, while in Europe the skill probably reached its height in terms of craftsmanship and innovation in Medieval times. Many of the stitches once worked have been forgotten and remain for the modern stitcher to rediscover, but there are numerous stitches that are still commonly worked today.

This book explains how to work 48 of these stitches, giving a wide selection that is more than enough to complete any project. Each stitch is explained in simple terms, with step-by-step illustrations to show you exactly what happens at every stage. There is also a sample of each stitch alongside its instructions and there are 16 designs, which together incorporate all the stitches so you can see them in use. If you need inspiration on using your designs you'll find plenty of ideas in the section on pages 16–23. Here you will find details on making a gorgeous evening bag, towel band and lavender sachet.

In this book the stitches are listed alphabetically, making it quick to find a particular stitch, and you'll also find information about what each stitch is used for: outlines, fillings, borders, specific shapes and so on. That way, if you want to design your own motifs or adapt the

■ *The Topiary design on page 53 uses satin stitch, split stitch buttonhole stitch bar and French knots as well as the less familiar overcast stitch and raised rose. It would make a wonderful design for a card, framed picture or scented sachet.*

ones in this book you'll get the help you need. When stitch variations are included, such as open fishbone stitch (page 44) they are placed beside the original stitch, in this case fishbone stitch.

Please read the advice about materials and equipment on the following pages along with the section on working the embroidery (pages 14–15), which should help to ensure your success. As with any craft it helps if you are working with the right equipment and know how to use it to best advantage.

Materials and Equipment

One of the wonders of embroidery is that it enables you to create beauty out of very little, without requiring a lot of tools, materials, workspace or expense. You can work nearly anywhere, even on a train, and when you have finished a session your embroidery can be tidied away in a bag or a drawer.

Fabric

This is your starting point with any design, and it doesn't have to be boring. You can work on literally any fabric from hessian to velvet, although beginners will find it easiest to work on a close-weave cotton or linen. Your choice of fabric will depend on the purpose of the embroidery and the effect you wish to achieve, as well as personal taste.

Linen or cotton is the classic embroiderer's fabric and an excellent choice for beginners. These fabrics handle well and have a regular weave that is a delight to work on. Being subtle, they allow the embroidery to take centre stage. Choose the best quality you can afford and if the finished item is likely to be cleaned then wash the fabric before you begin stitching to pre-shrink it.

Evenweave fabric, which has the same number of warp and weft threads and a regular pattern of holes between them, is really designed for counted thread work such as Hardanger embroidery, cross stitch, pulled thread embroidery and blackwork. However, you can work freestyle embroidery successfully on the higher counts (28 and above). On the lower counts this fabric is limiting because you have to follow the holes in the fabric.

Silk gives the embroidery a lavish, exotic look. You can work on fine silks, but for most purposes a firm silk such as washed silk, thick habutai, dupion, raw silk or taffeta are best. Combine with thread that has a silky finish such as Anchor Marlitt.

Plain weave fabrics in any fibre, including the classic cotton and linen (see left), have a smooth, tightly woven finish that is ideal for most surface embroidery. Choose something firm enough to support the embroidery well. Most embroidery threads combine attractively with plain weave fabrics including stranded cotton (floss), coton à broder and metallics.

Patterned fabrics are not the obvious choice but can combine well with freestyle embroidery. You can use embroidery to enhance the existing fabric pattern or work in the spaces around it – this is particularly appropriate on checked or striped fabric.

Hoops or Frames

Although not strictly essential, these really do make a difference to the quality of your work. They hold the fabric flat and taut, making it much easier to attain an even tension and preventing fabric distortion. Ideally choose a size that gives you room to work the design easily and that feels comfortable in your hands. A hoop 20 or 25cm (8 or 10in) across should suit most designs. See page 12 for information on using a hoop or frame.

A **wooden embroiderer's hoop**, also known as a tambour frame, is the most popular choice. It has two rings, one inside the other, and works by trapping the fabric between them, using an adjustable screw to tighten the tension on the outer ring.

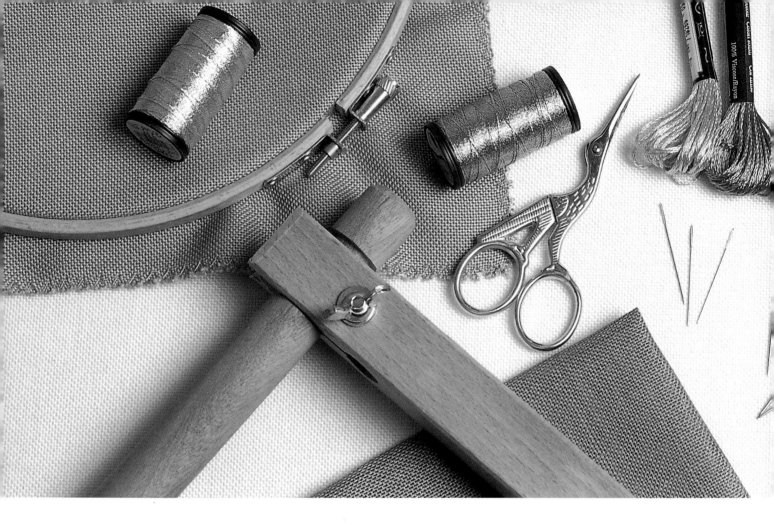

It is quick to fit and easy to use. The hoop must be larger than the design being worked because any embroidery caught between the two rings will be crushed and distorted. See page 12.

A **stretcher frame** is made from four wooden slats joined together to form a square or rectangle. The fabric can be stapled on to it to hold it taut. The disadvantage of this type of frame is that is not easy to re-adjust the tension of the fabric if it begins to slacken as work progresses.

An **upholstered frame** is like a stretcher frame except that it is more solid and has been covered with padding and fabric. The working fabric is simply pinned on to the frame and can be moved across as work progresses or if the tension needs adjustment.

A **rotating hand frame** is suitable for large designs and you won't need one for the projects in this book. It is a rectangular frame with a roller

at the top and bottom. The fabric is stretched between the rollers, with the excess fabric rolled around them neatly and the sides of the fabric are laced to the sides of the frame. The idea is that as the design progresses the fabric can be rolled on to expose a new area of fabric, ready to work.

Needles

You'll need a needle that has a larger eye than standard sewing needles to accommodate the thicker thread. The standard embroidery needle is called a crewel needle, but for certain work you may require a chenille or tapestry needle as well. Ideally buy a selection of sizes and choose a needle with a hole large enough for the thread to slide through without fraying but still fine enough to fit easily through the fabric. If your needles discolour look out for gold or platinum versions, which are more resistant to the chemicals in the skin.

Crewel needles are medium length with sharp points and large eyes and are ideal for fine to standard embroidery work. They come in sizes 0–10 with 0 being the largest. As a guide, use a No. 6 or No. 7 needle with three strands of embroidery thread and a No. 5 needle with all six strands. Use a No. 5 or No. 6 needle with Anchor Pearl Cotton No. 5.

Chenille needles are like crewel needles but with thicker stems. Use them when working with heavier threads or on coarse fabrics. For example, when working couching (page 38) you might use a chenille needle for the laid thread. They come in sizes 13–26, 13 being the largest.

Tapestry needles are useful for weaving threads through previously worked embroidery stitches because their blunt points won't pierce the fabric or catch the embroidery thread. For example, you will need one for ribbed wheel filling stitch (page 54).

Threads

Embroidery threads come in a vast range of colours and finishes, enabling you to do with thread everything an artist could achieve with paint and more.

Stranded cotton (floss) is the favourite choice for surface embroidery because it is highly versatile and has an attractive soft-sheen finish. Its six strands can be worked together or, as is usually the case, they can be separated into groups of three, two or even one strand for finer work. There are 472 colours in the Anchor range, including ombré and multi colours.

Anchor Pearl Cotton is a 2-ply, loosely cabled thread with a lovely sheen. It is available in several thicknesses –Anchor Pearl Cotton comes in sizes 3, 5, 8 and 12. It is a good choice when you want a raised or textured effect, as when working French knots (page 47), for example.

Anchor Coton à Broder is a 3-ply mercerized cotton with a lustrous finish. It is favoured for blackwork and whitework, but it can be used for any surface embroidery.

Anchor Marlitt is a 4-ply thread made from viscose/rayon that has a very high sheen and comes in 90 rich colours. Don't be mistaken into thinking that this is a synthetic thread. Viscose and rayon are made from wood pulp so they are still natural materials, and combine well with silk or cotton fabrics.

Anchor Pearl Metallic is used on the Christmas Stocking (page 55). It comes in white mingled with silver or gold, and red, green or blue mingled with gold or self-colour.

Metallic threads are available in a variety of colours and thicknesses. **Anchor Lamé** is a stranded metallic thread that can be used just like stranded cotton, but there are many other types of metallics available in a range of thicknesses that can be stitched or couched on to your work. Some of these can be quite fragile and have a gold covering around a core of thread. These are best used for laid work and couched in place.

Scissors

Ordinary household or paper scissors won't do for embroidery. You'll need a pair of dressmakers' scissors (shears) to cut the fabric to shape and another pair of small, fine-pointed scissors to trim off the ends of the embroidery threads close to the work.

Additional Equipment

You'll want a few other items to get started. Firstly you'll need to transfer the design to the fabric (see page 10). If you are using an embroidery hoop, you'll find it helps to bind the inner ring with cotton tape. You'll also need a measuring tape and may want a thimble and a needle threader.

Transferring a Design

There are several ways of transferring a design to fabric and each person will have his or her favourite. The easiest methods are tracing over a light source, using dressmakers' carbon paper, tacking or using iron-on transfers. No matter which method you use it is a good idea to cover all the marked lines with your stitching just in case they can't be completely removed, and will show on the finished piece.

Tracing Over a Light Source

TRACING OVER A LIGHT SOURCE is quick and easy to do. Ideally use a water-soluble embroidery marker, which will vanish away when the fabric is dampened. Tape the fabric over the design to make sure it does not shift while you are tracing.

■ *Correcting a Mistake*
If for any reason you make a mistake when using this method, it is easy to correct. Simply swill the fabric out in clean water to remove the marks, then dry and iron the fabric and start again.

Fig 1. Trace the outline of your design on to tracing paper with a fine black pen. Tape the tracing on to a light box or window and then tape your fabric on top, making sure the design is positioned correctly under the fabric.

Fig 2. Carefully go over the design lines with your water-soluble pen and then separate the layers. These lines will gradually fade, even from the moisture in the air, so do not set your partly worked embroidery aside for weeks and expect the lines to remain.

Using Dressmaker's Carbon Paper

DRESSMAKER'S CARBON PAPER can be used on any smooth fabric and is the best choice for coloured fabric because you can select a colour that really shows up. If the transferred line is faint in places it can be reinforced with ordinary pencil. You will need a tracing of your design.

Fig 1. Tape your fabric right side up on a flat surface and place the carbon paper coloured side down on top. Tape the traced design over it, making sure all layers are secure. Trace over the design with a hard pencil or ballpoint pen, pressing firmly and evenly.

Fig 2. Once you have gone over all the lines remove some of the tape and fold back the layers to reveal the fabric, making sure you do not disturb the position of the upper layers. If necessary, replace the upper layers and retrace any faint lines before separating the layers completely.

Tacking

Tacking (basting) is an easy method of transferring a design, but it works best with fairly simple patterns – with an intricate design you will find it takes far too long to tack over all the lines. It has the great advantage that it leaves no mark on the fabric.

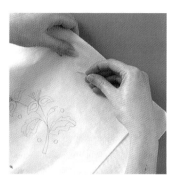

Fig 1. Trace your design onto tissue-grade paper that tears easily. Don't be tempted to use tracing paper or ordinary paper because it will be so hard to tear off that it may distort or break the tacking stitches. Pin the tracing over the fabric, right side facing up.

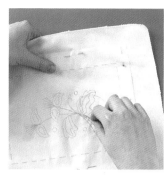

Fig 2. Tack (baste) the paper to the fabric around the edge to secure it, using sewing thread. With the same thread work lines of straight stitches (page 60) over each design line, starting with a knot on the top of the work. Keep the stitches fairly small, especially around curves.

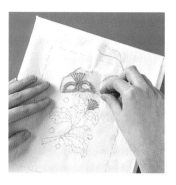

Fig 3. When all the design lines have been covered, tear off the paper and begin the embroidery. For a medium to large design you can remove the paper only from the part of the design you wish to work, leaving the paper in place over the remainder to keep the fabric clean.

Using Iron-On Transfers

Iron-on transfers of embroidery designs are available from embroidery and craft shops or you can make your own using a transfer pencil. This method is unsuitable for fabrics that can't be ironed hot, such as synthetics, or for very intricate designs because the lines tend to spread a little.

Fig 2. Place your transfer over the fabric, with the transfer side face down. Press down on the design with a hot iron, taking care not to move the iron as this could result in smudging.

Fig 1. To make your own transfer, tape tracing paper over your design and use a sharp pencil to trace over it. Flip the tracing over and draw over the design lines again, this time with a sharp transfer pencil. Press firmly and work on a hard surface.

Using a Hoop or Frame

An embroidery hoop or frame is essential for any medium to large embroidery project and usually worthwhile on even the smallest design. Having chosen the type you prefer, you now need to prepare it and mount your fabric correctly. Here are instructions for using the three main types of frame.

■ *An embroidery hoop or frame reduces the occurrence of puckering and helps to keep stitching tension even by holding the fabric smooth and flat. The piece on the near left was worked without a hoop and is still puckered even after framing. The design far left was worked in a hoop.*

Using an Embroidery Hoop

AN EMBROIDERY HOOP is inexpensive, easy to use and quick to fit or adjust. Hoops come in a variety of sizes and are light to hold. The work should be removed after each working session to avoid marking or stretching around the frame area. Binding the inner hoop helps hold the fabric more securely and prevents it marking the fabric.

Fig 1. Tape the end of some bias binding or cotton tape to the inner frame at a 45-degree angle. Wrap the binding around the frame, keeping it tight and overlapping it to prevent any gaps. When you reach the beginning, pin the binding in place and cut off the excess. Stitch the ends together securely and remove the pin.

Fig 2. Check that the fabric covers the hoop amply then prepare it for framing by working machine zigzag around the edges or trimming with pinking shears. Lightly press with a steam iron, if necessary, to remove creases.

Fig 3. Place the bound hoop on a firm surface and lay the fabric right side up on top. Slip the outer hoop over the other layers, sandwiching the fabric in the centre. Gently pull the sides of the fabric to remove any slack, if necessary, and then tighten the tension screw to hold the fabric securely.

Using a Stretcher Frame

STRETCHER FRAMES hold the fabric securely and are easy to hold but it takes time to mount the fabric correctly and the staples or drawing pins can damage the edges of the fabric. It is also very difficult to alter the tension.

Fig 1. Measure your frame and cut the fabric so that it is large enough to wrap around to the back. Iron the fabric to remove any creases. Lay out the fabric, place the frame on top and use a staple gun or drawing pins to attach the centre of each edge to the back of the frame. Make sure the fabric is taut.

Fig 2. If the fabric is not tight enough, remove the staples or drawing pins and adjust. When you are happy with the tension, work along the top of the frame, stapling or pinning the fabric in place and then pull the fabric tight and repeat along the bottom edge. Repeat to attach the fabric to the sides.

Using a Rotating Hand Frame

ROTATING HAND FRAMES are ideal for really large projects but they are not the best choice for small designs because it takes a long time to mount the fabric and you may need to use a lot of extra fabric to fit the frame. Look out for the new easy clip frames. With these the fabric is clipped to the rollers instead of stitched, making them quick to fit.

Fig 1. Cut the fabric to fit the frame. It should be no wider than the webbing on the rollers but at least as long as the sides. Neaten the edges of the fabric by stitching with machine zigzag, hemming or oversewing.

Fig 2. Pin the ends of the fabric to the webbing on the rollers, then stitch the fabric securely to the webbing and remove all pins. Make sure the fabric grain is straight. Take up the slack in the fabric by turning the rollers outwards and then tighten the rollers.

Fig 3. To secure the sides of the fabric lace them over the arms of the frame. Take a stitch in the fabric, then take the thread over and under the adjacent frame arm and take another stitch. Repeat to the end. The fabric should be taut in the frame.

Working the Embroidery

Once you have learnt how to start and finish your embroidery thread you can get under way. Everything else is just a matter of practice, trial and error. Keep your stitching tension as even as possible throughout and don't be afraid to add in some extra guidelines to help you work the more complicated stitches.

Starting Your Work

Cut a length of thread 45cm (18in) or less because longer lengths can knot, separate or fray. When using metallic thread use even less because this type of thread is more fragile. If you are using stranded cotton (floss) you may need to divide the threads. If so, cut the thread to length before separating it.

It is desirable to have the minimum of knots and trailing threads on the back of the work because even when the back will not be on view knots can cause lumps and trailing threads can show up as shadows on the right side.

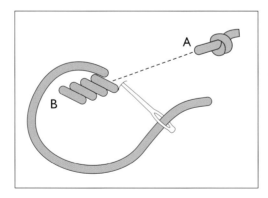

Start a new thread by making a knot in the end and passing the needle through the fabric from right side to wrong side at A, about 4 or 5cm (2in) beyond your starting point (B). Work the stitches back towards the knot, covering the thread on the back of the work and then cut off the knot. If necessary, work several elements of your design to ensure that the loose thread is secured before cutting off the knot. Once the design begins to fill up you can start a new thread by running it through the back of the completed stitching and then bringing it to the right side, ready to begin.

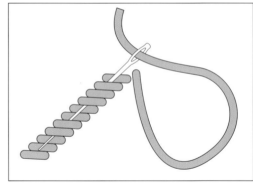

Finish your stitching by weaving the needle through the back of the stitching and snip off the thread end with sharp embroidery scissors.

For a **small, individual stitch** such as a French knot (page 47) or bullion stitch (page 26) start with a small knot on the back of the fabric. On completing the stitch pierce the thread just above the knot on the wrong side of the fabric. Pull the thread most of the way through, leaving a loop. Pass the needle through the loop to make a securing knot and trim off the thread end.

Importance of Tension

The key to successful embroidery is keeping the stitches the same length and maintaining an even tension. This is really a matter of practice. If you are using a new stitch or working one that you haven't used for some time it is always a good idea to work a trial piece on a scrap of your fabric before you begin on the embroidery. Time spent doing this will help raise the standard of your embroidery and save time unpicking mistakes. Work as many test stitches as it takes to start producing an even line. This may be as few as four or five. You hand will 'remember' the movement and the stitching on your embroidery will be correct from the start.

Using Guidelines

There are two types of guidelines you may need for your embroidery: the outline of the design and additional guidelines for particular stitches that you will probably need to mark on yourself. The latter can either be added to the fabric when the design is being transferred on to it or just before you work the stitch.

Design outlines should always be transferred to the fabric before you begin, even if you want to work a fairly loose, spontaneous design. This ensures a good balance between the design elements and maintains the scale throughout.

Additional guidelines are very useful for certain stitches, and even if you are an experienced embroiderer you may find these invaluable. When working feather stitch (page 40), for example, your design may only include the outer edges but it is helpful to mark additional guidelines one-third and two-thirds of the way across the stitch area to ensure that all the stitches are even. Stitches that overlap, such as flat stitch (page 46), open fishbone (page 44) and leaf stitch (page 48) also benefit from additional guidelines to ensure a really smooth result.

■ *The designs in this book are provided as bold outline drawings, as for the Poppies below (see page 33), allowing you to fill them with whatever combination of stitches you like. However, when working an overlapping stitch, such as flat stitch (shown below and on page 46), it is helpful to mark additional guidelines to indicate where stitches overlap. This ensures an even, professional-looking end result.*

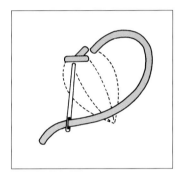

Embroidery Ideas

One of the advantages of freestyle or surface embroidery is that you can stitch where you want and on just about any fabric you like, giving you almost limitless creative possibilities. For many people the starting point is a small item such as a card, framed picture (see page 22) or sachet (page 21) and any of the designs in this book could be adapted for this type of use. However, because you can stitch on any fabric you can also work on an existing item. For example, you could stitch a group of flowers and leaves from Herbal Tea (page 59) on the corner of a tray cloth or pillowcase or stitch a fish from Underwater Garden (page 41) on a bathrobe.

Another interesting idea for a beginner is to take a motif that you like, such as a butterfly from the design on page 35, and stitch it at random over a large item – a tablecloth, pillowcase, curtain or duvet cover, for example. Stitch the motif at different angles and change the stitches you use for each area each time so that every motif is different but they all coordinate. This can be very satisfying and it is an excellent way of discovering the potential of every stitch and finding new ways to use it.

All of the designs in this book are less than 15cm (6in) high, so they won't take long to work and they will fit many applications. In addition, because they are worked from simple line drawings, they are easy to enlarge or reduce on a photocopier, giving them even greater versatility. Why not enlarge the Strawberries (page 45) for a tablecloth or the rose from the Topiary design (page 53) for a gardening outfit, for example?

For special occasions nothing beats the personal touch of embroidery, and if you have an important dinner or wedding to attend you will certainly impress your companions with an embroidered outfit or accessory. The embroidered bag shown right and on page 18 is a lovely accessory that will go with any outfit. It is deceptively simple to make and if desired you can work any of the designs in this book as an alternative to the one shown. Don't be afraid to try out your own ideas – freestyle embroidery is all about experimentation.

■ *This stunning evening bag will turn a few eyes green with envy, but it is quite straightforward to make. It is made in luxurious silk with gold ribbon and gold cord trims for that extra touch of glamour. See page 18 for instructions.*

Evening Bag

This evening bag can be made from satin or silk fabrics, depending on your preference. Silk should be dry cleaned only, so for practicality you may prefer a synthetic satin fabric. Choose colours to match a particular outfit or work on a neutral combination such as silver or gold and white or dramatic black and cream.

Materials

- 50cm (½yd) satin or silk fabric
- 30cm (12in) square of silk or satin fabric for the embroidery
- Anchor Stranded Cotton (floss) and Anchor Marlitt, as listed in the key on page 37
- 1m (1yd) of gold cord
- 1m (1yd) of gold ribbon 2.5cm (1in) wide
- Gold polyester thread and thread to match the fabrics
- Needles, pins and scissors

Bag Options

If you don't have use for an evening bag, you could utilize this super design to make a make-up bag, wash bag or jewellery holder. You could even use it to keep delicate items of clothing in or make one as a gift bag for a special present.

Work the Floral Garland design from page 37 or the design of your choice in the centre of your fabric square. Trace the bag pattern A given right and cut it from the embroidered fabric, keeping the design centred. Cut a second bag A for the back, either from the same fabric as the embroidery or from your other fabric. Cut two further bag pieces from your other fabric for the lining.

Pin the band (B) to the fabric and cut it out four times (or twice from folded fabric), so that you have two pieces for the bag and two pieces for the lining. With right sides facing, pin one band B to the embroidered bag piece with straight edges matching. Repeat for the bag back and the two bag linings and stitch the seams taking a 1cm (⅜in) seam allowance and using matching thread. Press the seams open.

With right sides together pin and then stitch the front and back bag pieces together, leaving the top edge of the band open. Snip into the seam allowances around the curve of the lower section and press the seams open with a warm iron. Repeat with the lining.

Turn the bag right side out. Fold the top 1cm (⅜in) to the wrong side and press with a warm iron. Leave the lining inside out. Fold the top 1cm (⅜in) to the wrong side on the lining

and press too. Slide the lining into the bag. Pin the two seams together at the bag opening so that the raw edges are sandwiched in between. If necessary, tuck in a little extra on the bag lining to get a good fit. Join the lining to the outer bag by stitching around the top of the bag just inside the edge.

Create a casing at the top of the bag by pining a 16cm (6¼in) length of gold ribbon to the front of the bag with one long edge level with the top of the bag. Repeat on the back. Tuck in the raw ends of the ribbons where they meet at the side seam and then stitch along each long edge; do not stitch across the ends of the ribbons. Thread the gold cord between the ribbon and the bag so that both ends emerge at the same side seam. Knot together. Cover the ends of the cord with small pieces of ribbon for added detail.

Shrink Prevention

To prevent silk from shrinking, pre-shrink it before you begin by steaming it with an iron set on hot. Do not touch the fabric with the iron, but hold it above the fabric and shoot out several blasts of steam. Leave to dry.

CUT 2 × FABRIC
CUT 2 × LINING FABRIC

BAG A

CUT 2 × FABRIC
CUT 2 × LINING FABRIC

BAND B

Dandelion Towel Band

Materials

- One guest towel
- 30cm (12in) square of satin
- Anchor Stranded Cotton (floss) and Anchor Marlitt, as listed in the key on page 43
- 2m (2yds) olive green ribbon 1cm (3/8in) wide
- 2m (2yds) of white ribbon 2.5cm (1in) wide
- Gold thread and white polyester thread
- Four metallic or pearl beads (optional)
- Needles, pins and scissors

A guest towel looks really special when it has been embroidered. Usually this is done on an attached band, but if you use the method here you can attach a panel to any part of the towel, and it can be whatever shape suits your embroidery design. The ribbon trims cover the raw edges of the fabric for a tidy finish that's easy to achieve.

Pre-wash and iron the towel. Stitch the Dandelions design from page 43 in the centre of the satin fabric or select any of the other designs in this book. Press the back lightly with a warm iron, then trim the fabric to leave a small border around all the edges of the design. Centre the embroidery over the towel close to the woven band near one end and stitch in place taking a 1cm (3/8in) seam allowance.

Cut the white and green ribbon to fit the side edges of the embroidery. Pin the white ribbon to the towel, covering the raw side edges of the embroidery and stitch in place close to each long edge. Pin a piece of green ribbon to the centre of each white ribbon and stitch down the centre with gold thread.

Repeat this process to cover the top and bottom edges of the embroidered fabric, this time taking the ribbons right up to the edges of the towel. Leave a little extra at each end, and turn this in before stitching the ribbon in place for a neat finish.

Make two small bows from the remaining ribbon pieces and stitch them to the base of the embroidery as a finishing touch. Sew a bead to the centre of each dandelion and one to the centre of the bow to finish.

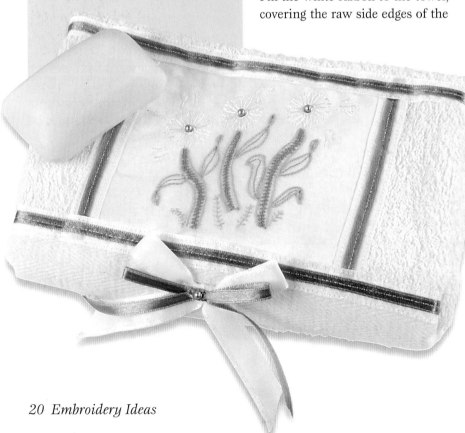

Alternative Designs

Any of the designs in this book could be used in this way. Choose a design that can be worked in the colours of the bathroom or select a multi-coloured design such as Underwater Garden (page 41) that would fit in anywhere.

Lavender Sachet

Lavender sachets are a luxurious addition to any bedroom closet, or you can pop one in your suitcase to keep it smelling sweet. This one is 13cm (5in) square, large enough to display any of the embroideries in this book, and is certain to keep its scent for months, if not years to come.

Materials

- Dried lavender
- Four 15cm (6in) squares of white fabric
- One 25cm (10in) square of silk organza
- Anchor Stranded Cotton (floss) as listed in the key on page 49
- 1m (1yd) of silver braid
- 1m (1yd) of white ribbon 2.5cm (1in) wide
- Three small glass beads that coordinate with the embroidery
- White polyester thread
- Needles, pins and scissors

Pre-wash the white fabric. When dry, press with a warm iron. Silk organza should be dry cleaned only. To pre-shrink it, see the tip on page 18. Embroider the Lavender Bouquet from page 49 in the centre of the organza and then cut the fabric into a 13cm (5in) square.

Centre the organza over one white fabric square and machine stitch around the edge of the organza, taking a 1cm (3/8in) seam and stitching through both layers. Pin and then stitch the white ribbon over the raw edge of the organza, mitring the corners, if desired.

With right sides facing, pin another white square to the organza. Trim to match, if necessary. Stitch around the edges taking a 1cm (3/8in) seam allowance and leaving a small opening in one side to turn through. Trim the seams and turn the sachet right side out.

Make another little sachet from the two remaining pieces of white fabric, taking a slightly wider seam allowance to make this one slightly smaller. Turn this sachet right side out and stuff with dried lavender. Slipstitch the opening in the seam closed. Carefully slide the lavender-filled bag into the embroidered sachet and slipstitch the side opening closed.

Hand stitch the silver braid over the machine stitching line on the white ribbon and make a small loop at the top to hang the sachet from, if required. Finish by sewing three small glass beads into the centre of the bow in the hanging loop.

Substitute the Filling

If you haven't got any dried lavender you can use potpourri or stuff the inner sachet with polyester filling sprinkled with a few drops of your favourite essential oil.

Framing Your Work

Framing is an excellent way of presenting any of the designs in this book. It enables you to display your work without the risk of it being damaged by excessive handling and preserves it for future generations. You can frame it yourself or pay for it to be done professionally, but even if you choose the latter route it is worth doing the preparatory work yourself, lacing it to a backing board to ensure that it is crease free. A layer of thin wadding (batting) behind the embroidery gives it added protection and helps to produce a smooth look.

Preparing Your Embroidery for Framing

To centre your embroidery exactly in the frame it helps to have an equal border around the edge of the design. Take the dimensions of the frame and add 5–10cm (2–4in) depending on the size of the embroidery. This is the size you want your fabric to be. Measure out to each side from the centre of the fabric by half the calculated width and mark this with a pencil. Then measure out from the centre by half the calculated height and again mark the fabric. Draw lines between the marks to create a border. Check your measurement by centring the backing of the frame over the design. You should have a 2.5–5cm (1–2in) border of fabric all round the backing frame. Check that the design is centred within your drawn frame and that the fabric grain is straight. Trim the fabric along your drawn line.

Now when you lace your embroidery (see below) it should be easy to centre it on the padded board. If desired, you can also draw or tack the fabric where the edges of the board will be to help position it easily and correctly. Although this may seem like extra effort, it makes the next stage much quicker as well as reducing the possibilities of error.

When you are ready for framing check that the frame and glass are clean and dry on both sides, with no smears on the glass. Lace your embroidery to the board following the instructions below and then fit it neatly in the frame. Seal the back with gummed paper tape, pressing it gently into the rebate. The tape will shrink as it dries, sealing in the picture and helping to keep out dust and tiny insects.

Lacing Your Work

LACING YOUR WORK stretches it taut and ensures that it will be held neatly in the frame. Use foamcore board, which has a layer of polystyrene sandwiched between layers of thin card, because this enables you to pin the embroidery to the edges. Make sure that you centre your embroidery exactly on the card and use padding to smooth over any lumps.

Fig 1. Cut foamcore board and polyester wadding (batting) to fit your chosen frame and attach the wadding to the card using glue stick or double-sided tape. Leave to dry. Lay out your embroidery, face down, and centre the padded board on top.

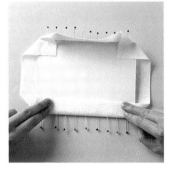

Fig 2. Secure the fabric by pinning into the sides of the foamcore board, working first along one edge and then along the opposite edge. Flip the embroidery over and check that the design is centred. When you are happy with the positioning, flip it back over, fold in the corners diagonally and then pin the remaining sides in place.

Fig 3. The edges of a small design can be secured with double-sided tape. For a larger design lace opposite edges together with strong thread in a large needle, taking a stitch first on one side and then on the other. Pull the thread tight every few stitches. Repeat to lace the remaining opposite sides together. Oversew the mitred corners to finish.

Antwerp Edging

ANTWERP EDGING (knot stitch edging) is similar to buttonhole stitch (page 28) but with a bold knot on the outside edge, as shown on the design opposite. Work the stitches an even width apart.

■ *Easy Alternative*

Antwerp edging is a difficult stitch to work, requiring care and patience. If you haven't worked it before, work a test piece on scrap fabric first or consider working buttonhole stitch as an easier alternative.

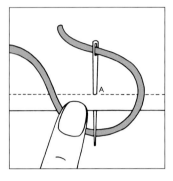

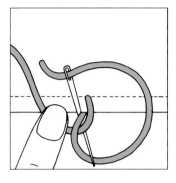

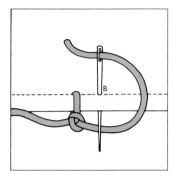

Fig 1. Hold down the thread end with your thumb and insert the needle from the right side at A, keeping the working thread under the needle.

Fig 2. Still holding the thread end down, pull the working thread to form a twisted loop, then pass the needle behind the loop, keeping the working thread under the needle, as shown.

Fig 3. Pull the thread firmly to set the knot and insert the needle at B, ready to work the next stitch. Darn in the thread ends between the layers of the hem.

Back Stitch

BACK STITCH is an outlining stitch, producing a solid line that will bend around curves when the stitches are quite short. In the design opposite it is used to outline the cake.

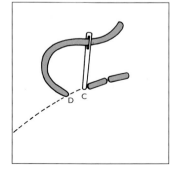

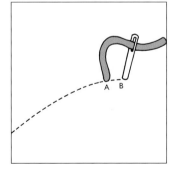

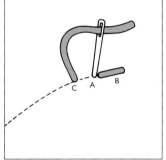

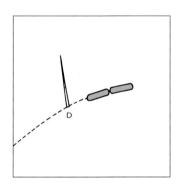

Fig 1. Bring the needle through at A, one stitch length from the start of the line, and insert it at B, at the beginning.

Fig 2. Bring the needle out at C so that A lies halfway between B and C, and re-insert it at A in the hole previously made.

Fig 3. Bring the needle out at D, making sure you maintain the same stitch length as before.

Fig 4. Re-insert the needle at C, in exactly the same hole as previously made, and then continue in the same way. To go around tight curves you may need to make the stitch length slightly shorter.

ANCHOR STRANDED
COTTON (FLOSS)

50

1304 (multicolor)

ANCHOR MARLITT

820   1077

ANCHOR PEARL MULTICOLOR NO. 8

1344

FINISHED SIZE
11.5 x 11cm (4½ x 4¼in)

Stitching Notes

Celebration Cake
Work this pretty cake with two strands of thread unless otherwise stated. Use back stitch to outline the cake in 50 and Antwerp edging in 1077 to indicate the cloth it is resting on. Stitch the candles in bullion stitch with individual chain stitches in 820 for the flames. Use herringbone stitch in 1344 to decorate the sides of the cake with a single raised rose on the centre tier, flanked by swirls of stem stitch. For the flowers use French knots in 1304. Work the balloons (using one strand) and their strings (two strands) in stem stitch with satin stitch in 820 for the highlights. Work the stars on the background with straight stitches in 1077.

Bokhara Couching

Bokhara couching creates a thick, dense filling or can be used as an outline stitch. With most couching one thread is laid across the fabric and then a second, finer thread is used to stitch it down. With Bokhara couching the same thread is used for both (see also Romanian couching, page 56). Bokhara couching is used for the frame in the design opposite.

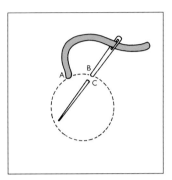

Fig 1. Bring the needle out at A, insert it at B and bring it out again at C.

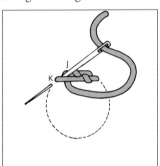

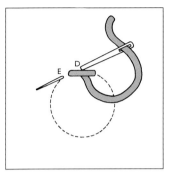

Fig 2. Insert the needle at D to trap the laid thread with a slanting stitch, and bring it out at E, ready to lay another thread.

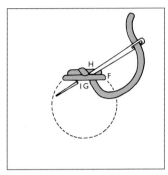

Fig 3. Insert the needle at F and bring it out at G then insert it at H and bring it out at I.

Fig 4. Insert the needle at J and bring it out at K, ready to lay another thread. Notice how the catching stitches are staggered to enable them to lie neatly and to create an attractive pattern. If desired, the couching stitches can be spaced quite wide apart as in the design opposite. Continue in the same way.

Bullion Stitch

Bullion stitch is an individual stitch that can be grouped to form a motif such as a flower. Work it like a French knot (page 47) but with more twists around the needle. It is used for the 'tassel' in the design opposite.

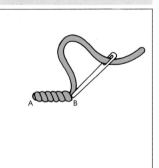

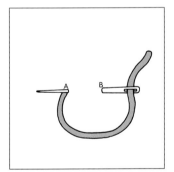

Fig 1. Bring the needle out at A, at the start of the stitch. Insert it at the end point, B, and then bring it out again at A. Do not pull the needle right through the fabric.

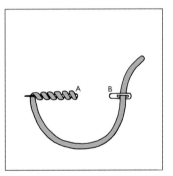

Fig 2. Twist the thread around the needle point five or six times so it will cover the length between A and B.

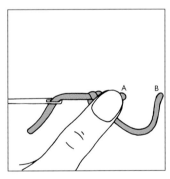

Fig 3. Place your thumb on the coiled thread and pull the needle through, taking care not to distort the twists.

Fig 4. Insert the needle at B and pull the working thread until the bullion stitch lies flat.

KEY

ANCHOR STRANDED
COTTON (FLOSS)

 254   1215

403   9046

901

ANCHOR MARLITT

1077   1078

ANCHOR PEARL COTTON
METALLIC

7001

FINISHED SIZE
11.5 x 8cm (4½ x 3in)

Stitching Notes

Japanese Lady

Work this design with one strand of thread unless otherwise stated. For the outer gold frame work Bokhara couching in 1078. Inside this couch on two strands of 7001 individually and work a further border of chevron stitch within that in 1077. Around the inner edge of the frames work a line of stem stitch and use the same stitch for the lady's face. Using two strands of thread, stitch her hair in satin stitch. Work her robe, including the bands at the top, in split stitch. Work the pins in her hair in straight stitch with a French knot at the end of each. Use satin stitch with bullion stitches at the ends for the tassels.

Buttonhole Stitch

BUTTONHOLE STITCH is an edging stitch that can also be worked as an outline or in a circle to create wheels. In the Christmas Cottage on page 31 it is used for the grass and bushes.

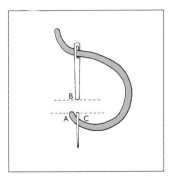 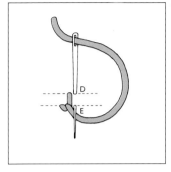 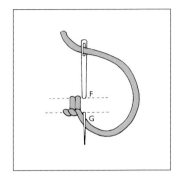

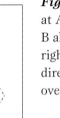

Fig 1. Bring the needle out at A. Insert the needle at B above and slightly to the right, and bring it out at C, directly below, passing it over the working thread.

Fig 2. Pull the thread through to form the stitch. Insert the needle at D and bring it out at E, directly below, with the thread under the needle.

Fig 3. Continue working stitches as shown, keeping the stitch height and spacing as even as possible.

Fig 4. The stitches should usually be worked close together, but when working around curves allow the top edge to fan out slightly.

Buttonhole Stitch Bar

BUTTONHOLE STITCH BARS are traditionally used for linking areas of cutwork, but they can also be used in freestyle embroidery. They are used to embellish the Christmas tree in the design on page 31.

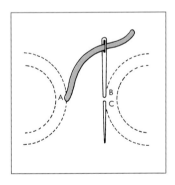 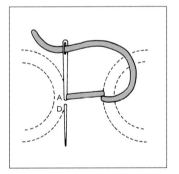 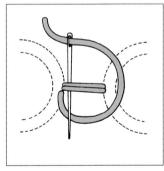

Fig 1. Bring the needle out at A, at the start of the bar. Insert the needle at B, at the end of the bar, and take a small downward stitch, bringing the needle out at C.

Fig 2. Insert the needle again at A and bring it out at D, just below A.

Fig 3. Pass the needle down behind the bar you have made, passing it over the working thread, as shown here.

Fig 4. Pull the thread taut but not so tight that it distorts the bar and then repeat step 3 until you have covered the entire bar. Finish the thread end at the back of the work.

Knotted Buttonhole Stitch

KNOTTED BUTTONHOLE STITCH is a decorative version of buttonhole stitch that has a knot at the top edge. It is used in the Christmas Cottage on page 31 for the red flowers in front of the house and tree.

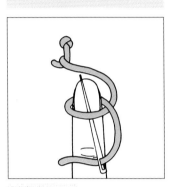

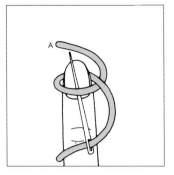

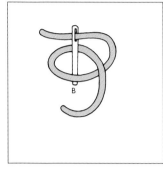

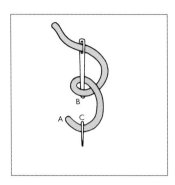

Fig 1. Bring the needle out at A, on the lower design line, and make a loop around your finger with the thread. Insert the needle up through the loop.

Fig 2. Slide your finger out and with the loop still around the needle, insert the needle at B, on the upper design line slightly to the right of A.

Fig 3. Bring the needle out at C, with the thread under the point and, before pulling the needle through, tighten the loop around it by pulling the thread.

Fig 4. Pull the needle through to form the stitch and then make a loop over your finger for the next stitch.

Up and Down Buttonhole Stitch

UP AND DOWN BUTTONHOLE STITCH is worked with the needle flowing in alternate directions, hence its name. It makes a pretty edging or outline and can be used in place of buttonhole stitch.

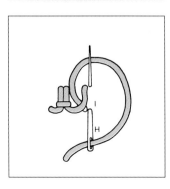

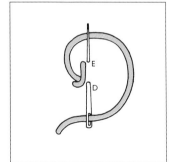

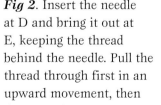

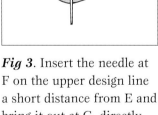

Fig 1. Bring the needle out at A on the lower design line. Insert the needle at B on the upper line and bring it out at C, immediately below. Keep the thread under the needle.

Fig 2. Insert the needle at D and bring it out at E, keeping the thread behind the needle. Pull the thread through first in an upward movement, then downwards.

Fig 3. Insert the needle at F on the upper design line a short distance from E and bring it out at G, directly below, as shown.

Fig 4. Insert the needle at H, next to G and bring it out at I, then continue in the same way to complete the line of stitching. Keep the spaces between the stitches even.

Cable Stitch

CABLE STITCH makes a bold, solid outline stitch, but it can also be massed in rows as a filling stitch. It is used for the circular border around the Christmas Cottage, shown opposite.

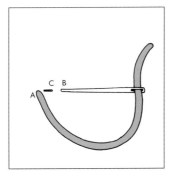

Fig 1. Bring the needle out at A, at the start of the stitching line. Keeping the thread below the needle, insert the needle at B, to the right of A and bring it out at C, midway between A and B.

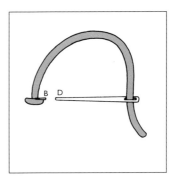

Fig 2. Work the next stitch in the same way, but this time keep the thread above the needle, inserting the needle at D and bringing it out at B.

Fig 4. Insert the needle at F and bring it out at E with the thread above the needle. Continue in the same way to the end of the line.

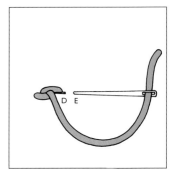

Fig 3. Insert the needle at E and bring it out at D, this time with the thread below the needle.

Cable Chain Stitch

CABLE CHAIN STITCH is an outline stitch that looks like chain stitch (page 32) but with a small link between each chain. Like cable stitch, above, it can also be worked in massed lines as a filling stitch or to create bands. It is used for the fence in the design opposite and worked individually (detached) for the flowers in the foreground.

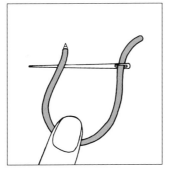

Fig 1. Bring the needle out at A and hold the thread down with your finger or thumb. Pass the needle from right to left under the working thread, without piercing the fabric.

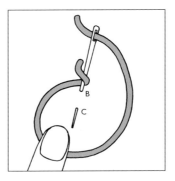

Fig 2. Twist the needle back to the right over the working thread and, still holding the thread, insert the needle at B, bringing it out at C. Keeping the thread under the needle, pull the working thread to form a chain loop.

Fig 3. Repeat the process to insert the needle at D and bring it out at E.

KEY

ANCHOR STRANDED COTTON (FLOSS)

227		403	
229		852	
254		907	
277		9046	

ANCHOR MARLITT

826		1078	
846		1079	

FINISHED SIZE
12.5 x 12.5cm (5 x 5in)

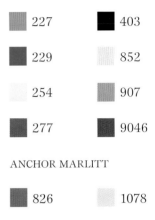

Stitching Notes

Christmas Cottage

Work this scene using two strands of thread unless otherwise stated. Use stem stitch to outline the house and fill with satin stitch, using straight stitch or herringbone for the window leading in 1078. Work the wall in split stitch and straight stitch with French knot flowers. Fill the tree with split stitch and add buttonhole stitch bars with straight stitch for the star. Use knotted buttonhole stitch for the red flowers and buttonhole stitch for the greenery. Work the fence wire in one strand of 826, using cable chain stitch. Work the front plants in cable chain stitch and French knots. Add a border of cable chain stitch.

Knotted Cable Chain Stitch

KNOTTED CABLE CHAIN STITCH is a lacy outline stitch worked like cable chain stitch (page 30) but with a decorative knot in each link. It is used in the design opposite for the poppy stems.

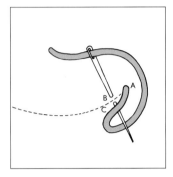

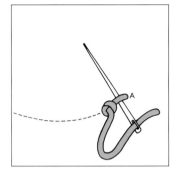

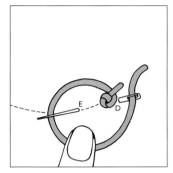

Fig 1. Bring the needle out at A and insert it at B, bringing it back out at C. Wrap the thread over and under the needle, as shown.

Fig 2. Pull the thread through and then slip the needle under the stitch between the knot and A, without piercing the fabric.

Fig 3. Pull the thread through, insert the needle at D and bring it out at E, with the thread under the needle. Hold the thread down with your finger or thumb. Pull through to form a chain.

Fig 4. Insert the needle at F and bring it out at G, then wrap the thread over and under the needle to start the next stitch. Continue, keeping the stitches even.

Chain Stitch

CHAIN STITCH can be used as an outline stitch or worked in rows as a lacy filling. It is made by working a series of looped stitches together in a line and it is simple yet satisfying. It is used for the wheat heads in the poppies design opposite.

■ *Even Tension*
Pull each stitch to the desired size as you work. The stitches are connected, so if you try to make one stitch a little larger later on, you'll find that you are pulling up one of the stitches next to it.

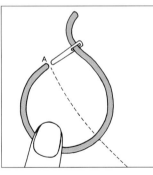

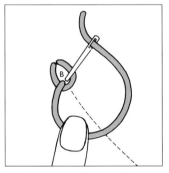

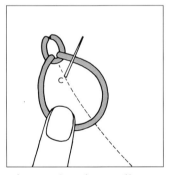

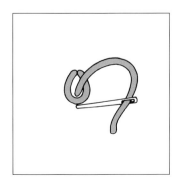

Fig 1. Bring the needle out at A, hold the thread down and insert the needle through the same hole.

Fig 2. Bring the needle out at B and, keeping the thread under the needle, pull the loop of thread to form a chain. Insert the needle through the same hole at B.

Fig 3. Bring the needle out at C for the next stitch.

Fig 4. Finish the final loop with a small tying stitch, as shown.

KEY

ANCHOR STRANDED
COTTON (FLOSS)

▦	225	▦	887
▦	227	▦	9046
■	403		

FINISHED SIZE

12.5 x 11cm (5 x 4 ¼ in)

Stitching Notes

Poppies

Use two strands of thread to stitch this design unless otherwise stated. Work the red poppy petals in satin stitch using 9046 and then outline them with stem stitch for added definition. Work the flower stamens with extended French knots using 403. Use knotted cable chain stitch for the stems of the poppies and the poppy buds in 227, then complete their heads with split stitch. Capture the texture of the wheat heads with chain stitch, adding straight stitches around the edges, and then work their stems with stem stitch all in 887. Use stem stitch for the fine grasses too.

Open Chain Stitch

OPEN CHAIN STITCH, also called square chain and ladder chain stitch, is a lacy outline or filling stitch that can be worked to various widths. In the design opposite its open appearance helps to suggest the translucency of the butterflies' wings.

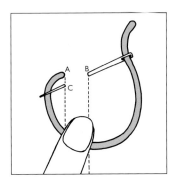

Fig 1. Bring the needle out at A and insert it to the right at B, bringing it back out at C. Hold the working thread down and under the needle, leaving the loop slightly loose.

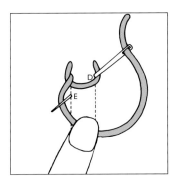

Fig 2. Insert the needle at D and bring it out at E, below C.

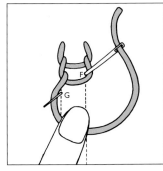

Fig. 3. Insert the needle at F and bring it out at G. Secure the last stitch with a small loop at each side.

Rosette Chain Stitch

ROSETTE CHAIN STITCH is another outline stitch that works well as a filling stitch. It can also be worked in a circle or ring. It forms an intricate looped line that can be worked slightly open for a lacy effect or close together for a dense, braid-like filling. In the design opposite it is used to outline the wings of the butterflies.

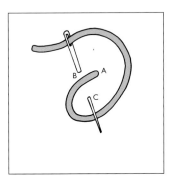

Fig 1. Bring the needle out at A and insert it at B, bringing it back out at C. Wrap the thread over and under the needle, as shown.

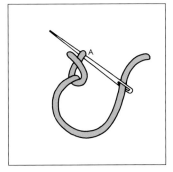

Fig 2. Pull the thread through to form a twisted loop and then slip the needle under the thread between the twist and A, without piercing the fabric.

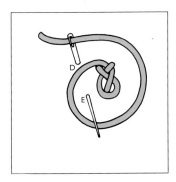

Fig 3. Pull the thread through, taking care not to tug too tightly. Insert the needle at D and bring it out at E. Continue working in sequence, spacing the stitches evenly.

ANCHOR STRANDED COTTON (FLOSS)

▦	50		300
▦	254	▥	1215

ANCHOR MARLITT

☐	800	▦	1078

FINISHED SIZE
13 x 12.5cm (5^1/8 x 5in)

Stitching Notes

Butterflies

Use one strand of thread for this design. First outline the butterflies in rosette chain stitch using 50. Outline the bodies and add the antennae with stem stitch. Fill the solid blocks on their wings and bodies with satin stitch, adding the wing veining with open chain stitch and buttonhole stitch bars. Add detail with 1078, using French knots on the antennae and straight stitch for the legs. Work the daisy head with satin stitch using 1078 for the centre and 800 for the petals and use stem stitch for the stem and leaf outlines in 254. For the leaf veins use 1215.

Twisted Chain Stitch

TWISTED CHAIN STITCH is a decorative outlining stitch, giving textural interest to simple designs. It is also ideal for suggesting the sinewy forms of vines and leaf tendrils as in the lovely Floral Garland design shown opposite.

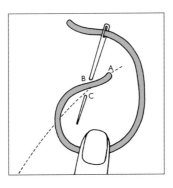

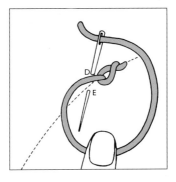

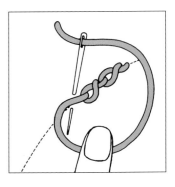

Fig 1. Bring the needle out at A and insert it to the side of the design line at B. Take a small, slanting stitch across the line and bring the needle out at C. Pass the thread over and then under the needle, as shown.

Fig 2. Gently pull the thread up to form a twisted chain and make sure it is the desired size. Insert the needle at D and bring it out at E, as shown.

Fig 3. Pull the thread through to form a twisted chain and then continue in the same way. Secure the final stitch with a small tying stitch in the same way as for chain stitch (page 32).

Chained Feather Stitch

CHAINED FEATHER STITCH can be worked as a border stitch or in pictorial designs, as shown opposite. When working a border mark both side edges before you start to avoid stitching off line.

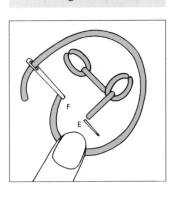

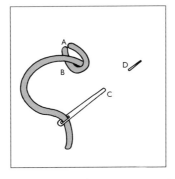

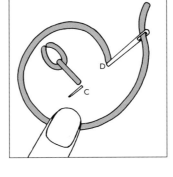

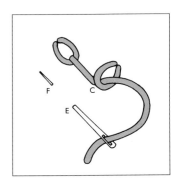

Fig 1. Bring the needle out at A and make a slanting chain stitch (see page 32), bringing the needle out at B. Take the needle in at C and bring it out at D, level with B.

Fig 2. Holding the thread down as shown, re-insert the needle at D and bring it out again at C.

Fig 3. Keeping the thread under the needle, pull the thread through and insert the needle at E (immediately below B) and bring it out at F (level with C and below A).

Fig 4. Take the needle in at F and bring it out at E then continue in the same way to complete the line of stitching.

KEY

ANCHOR STRANDED
COTTON (FLOSS)

■	63	■	1304 (multicolor)
■	131	■	1325 (multicolor)

ANCHOR MARLITT

■	813	■	1066
	820	■	1067
■	867		

FINISHED SIZE
12.5 x 12.5cm (5 x 5in)

Stitching Notes

Floral Garland

Work this design with one strand of thread unless otherwise stated. Use twisted chain stitch in 1067 for the climbing vine that outlines the motif, with chained feather stitch on the pale pink flowers, the overhanging wisteria flowers (1325) and the vine leaves (1066). Use spider's webs filling for the yellow climbing roses in 1304 and satin stitch for the irises in 131 with stem stitch stalks and satin stitch leaves in 1066. Use detached chain stitch for the yellow flowers (820) with French knots for their centres.

Chevron Stitch

CHEVRON STITCH is a zigzag border stitch that can also be worked as a filling. It can be worked open, as shown here, or closed, with the horizontal stitches sharing the same holes to create the effect of back stitch lines with zigzag lines in between. It is used in the Japanese Lady design on page 27 for the inside portion of the frame.

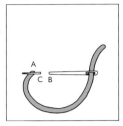

Fig 1. Bring the needle out at A on the lower design line, insert it at B and bring it out at C, halfway between A and B. Keep the thread below the needle, as shown.

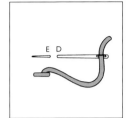

Fig 2. Insert the needle at D on the upper design line and take a small stitch to bring it out at E.

Fig 3. Insert the needle at F so that D is halfway between E and F. Keep the thread above the needle, and bring it out again at D.

Fig 4. Insert the needle at G on the lower design line and bring it out again at H.

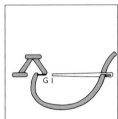

Fig 5. Insert the needle at I and bring it out at G. Continue in the same way to complete the line of stitching.

Couching

COUCHING is a means of utilizing a thicker, more decorative or delicate thread than you would be able to stitch with conventionally. This thread is simply laid on top of the fabric and secured with a finer, usually matching, thread or you can use the same thread for both. It is used around the edge of the Japanese Lady design on page 27.

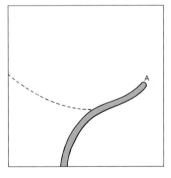

Fig 1. Bring the decorative thread through at A and lay it along the design line.

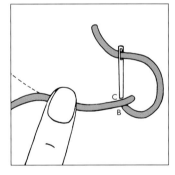

Fig 2. Hold the laid thread in position as you work, keeping it fairly taught. Bring the securing thread through at B and insert it at C on the opposite side of the laid thread.

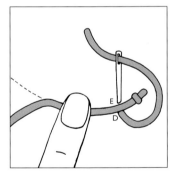

Fig 3. Bring the needle out at D and insert it at E. Continue until you have secured the entire length of laid thread. Take the laid thread through to the wrong side and finish off both threads.

Jacobean Couching

JACOBEAN COUCHING (trellis square filling) is a filling stitch that creates an open, basket-weave appearance, which makes an attractive contrast to denser filling stitches such as satin stitch or long-and-short stitch. Usually one thread is used for the laid straight stitches and a second thread for the securing stitches.

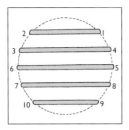

Fig 1. Work long, evenly spaced straight stitches (page 60) across the shape horizontally, as shown here.

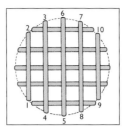

Fig 2. Repeat to work long, evenly spaced straight stitches over the shape, vertically.

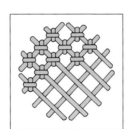

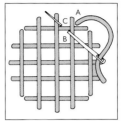

Fig 3. Bring the needle out at A, insert it at B, diagonally over the intersection of laid threads, and bring it out at C in readiness for the next stitch.

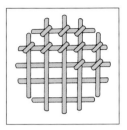

Fig 4. Continue working these half cross stitches, from right to left, then left to right on the next row.

Fig 5. Alternatively, work the straight stitches diagonally and tie them down with cross stitches, as shown.

Cretan Stitch

CRETAN STITCH is a filling stitch from the feather stitch family. Its open, plait-like appearance makes it excellent for filling leaf shapes as shown in the Herbal Tea design on page 59. It adds a lovely, tactile quality to your work.

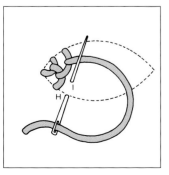

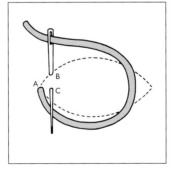

Fig 1. Bring the needle out at A and insert it at B, bringing it back out at C with the thread under the point of the needle.

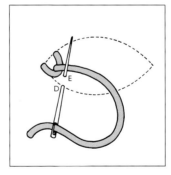

Fig 2. Pull the thread up to form a loop and insert the needle at D, bringing it out at E, with the thread under the point.

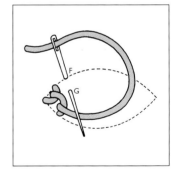

Fig 3. Continue as before, following the curve of the design, taking the needle down at F and out at G.

Fig 4. Take the needle in at H and out at I, then continue this double sequence to the end.

Double Knot Stitch

DOUBLE KNOT STITCH is also known as double coral knot, Palestrina knot, Smyrna knot and old English knot. It creates an ornate, chunky outline or it can be worked in rows as a filling stitch. It is used for the sea-bed in the design opposite.

Fig 1. Bring the needle out at A on the design line and insert it at B, bringing it back out at C to form a slanting stitch.

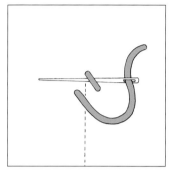

Fig 2. Pass the needle behind the stitch you have made without piercing the fabric, as shown.

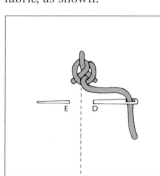

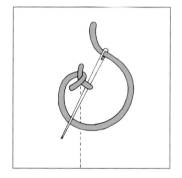

Fig 3. Pull the thread through. Pass the needle behind the lower half of the stitch, without piercing the fabric and keeping the thread under the needle, as shown. Pull the thread through to form a knot.

Fig 4. Insert the needle at D and bring it out at E, ready for the next stitch.

Feather Stitch

FEATHER STITCH was used to decorate work smocks in the 18th and 19th centuries, together with chain stitch and buttonhole stitch, and is still used to decorate hems. It can be used for outlines, as shown opposite, or for borders or fillings. Stitches are worked from top to bottom.

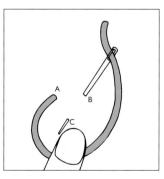

Fig 1. Bring the needle out at A and insert it at B on the same level, bringing it back out at C. A, B and C should be equidistant.

Fig 2. Insert the needle at D and bring it out at E, keeping the thread underneath. The distances between C, D and E should be the same.

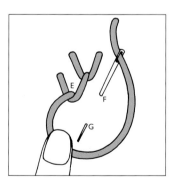

Fig 3. Continue working in this way, keeping the thread below the needle. At the end of a row take the thread over the last loop and finish off at the back.

KEY

ANCHOR STRANDED
COTTON (FLOSS)

	52		410
	225		886
	254		1201
	291		1325 (multicolor)

ANCHOR MARLITT

	820		1017

FINISHED SIZE
12 x 12.5cm (4¾ x 5in)

Stitching Notes

Underwater Garden

Work this design with two strands of thread unless otherwise stated. Use satin stitch for the starfish, yellow rocks (291) and fish, adding details to the fish with straight stitch and outlining them with stem stitch worked with a single strand of cotton. Add French knots to the centre of the starfish in 1325. Outline the anemones in straight stitch in 1201 with satin stitch filling, French knot details and extended French knots for their tentacles. Use feather stitch for the leafy seaweed and weave one strand between the stitches. For the sea bed use double knot stitch in 886 and for the round shapes work spider's web filling in 52.

Spanish Knotted Feather Stitch

SPANISH KNOTTED FEATHER STITCH is a variation of feather stitch that produces a much denser, ornate look. Use it for thick outlines or fillings. In the Dandelions design opposite it is used for the stem centres.

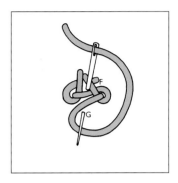

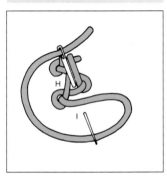

Fig 1. Bring the needle out at A, insert it at B and bring it through again at C. Wrap the thread over and under the needle, as shown.

Fig 2. Pull the thread through and insert the needle at D, bringing it out at E. Wrap the thread over and under the needle.

Fig 3. Pull the thread through and insert the needle at F, bringing it out at G. Wrap the thread over and under the needle.

Fig 4. Pull the thread through, insert the needle at H and bring it out at I. Wrap the thread over and under the needle. Pull the thread through and continue working in sequence, following figures 3 and 4.

Fern Stitch

FERN STITCH is an easy stitch that creates a lovely feathery effect, ideal for leaf forms. It can be worked as an outline or massed as a filling. In the design opposite it is used for the small ferns.

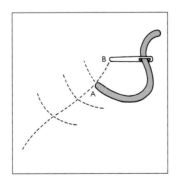

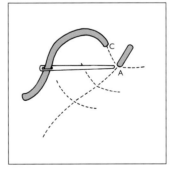

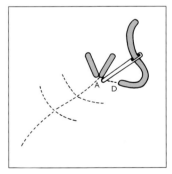

Fig 1. Bring the needle out at A and insert it at B.

Fig 2. Bring the needle out at C and then insert it at A, through the same hole as before, as shown.

Fig 3. Bring the needle out at D and re-insert it at A. This completes a single fern stitch.

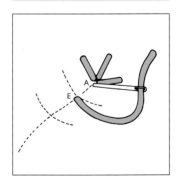

Fig 4. Bring the needle out at E and insert it at A. Continue in this way, following the design line.

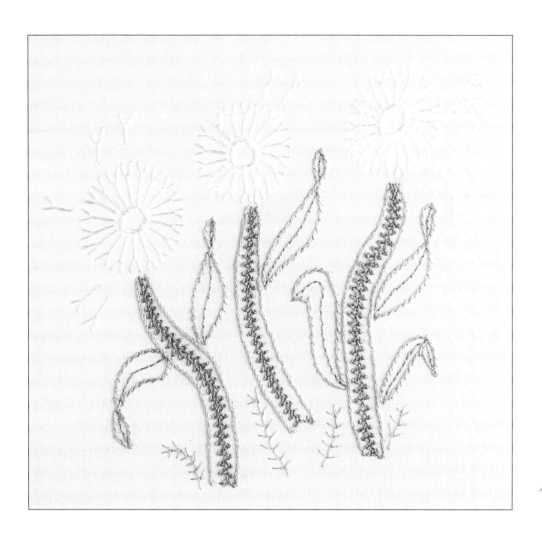

KEY

ANCHOR STRANDED
COTTON (FLOSS)

 214   215

ANCHOR MARLITT

 800

FINISHED SIZE
10 x 11cm (4 x 4¼in)

Stitching Notes

Dandelions

This design shows how fly stitch can be extended, here creating the seed heads. Use one strand of cotton (floss) or Marlitt throughout. Work the seed heads in fly stitch using 800, extending the tails approximately 1cm (³⁄₈in) towards the centre. Use stem stitch to define the round centres. Work the centre of the stems in Spanish knotted fern stitch using 215 and then outline them with stem stitch using 214. Work the leaf outlines in rope stitch with back stitch for the veins, all in 214. Finally, work the small ferns at the base of the dandelions with fern stitch.

Fishbone Stitch

FISHBONE STITCH is a filling stitch that is ideal for leaf shapes, as shown opposite. It interweaves at the centre, creating the leaf vein, and is angled so that the light catches the thread for a three-dimensional effect.

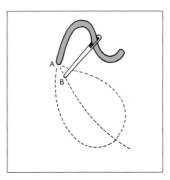

Fig 1. Bring the needle out at A and insert it at B, making a small straight stitch along the centre line of the shape.

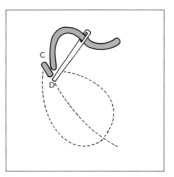

Fig 2. Bring the needle out at C and insert it at D next to the base of the first stitch, as shown.

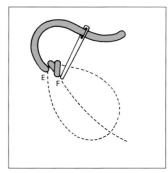

Fig 3. Bring the needle out at E and insert it at F, overlapping the base of the previous stitch, as shown.

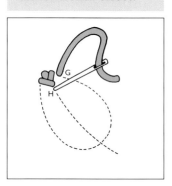

Fig 4. Bring the needle out at G and insert it at H, overlapping the base of the previous stitch. Cover the entire shape in this way, butting the stitches up tightly so that there are no gaps.

Open Fishbone Stitch

OPEN FISHBONE STITCH is basically fishbone stitch worked in an open pattern for a lacier effect but with the stitches overlapping at the centre. It can be used as an alternative to fishbone stitch when other elements have been worked with dense fillings to provide textural interest as in the Strawberries design, shown opposite.

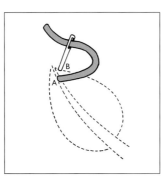

Fig 1. Bring the needle out at A and insert it at B to form a small sloping stitch.

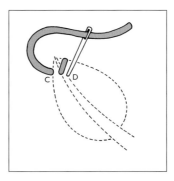

Fig 2. Bring the needle out at C and insert it at D.

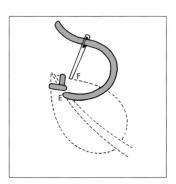

Fig 3. Bring the needle out at E and insert it at F. Continue in this way, working sloping stitches alternately on each side until the shape is filled, spacing stitches evenly.

KEY

ANCHOR STRANDED
COTTON (FLOSS)

�largecolor	35		301
■	245	▨	832
■	254	■	9046

ANCHOR MARLITT

■ 893

FINISHED SIZE
10.5 x 11.5cm (4⅛ x 4½ in)

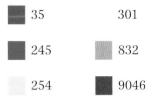

Stitching Notes

Strawberries
Use two strands of thread for this leafy design. Stitch the strawberries with split stitch in all three reds, adding highlights in 301. Work the seeds of the strawberries with French knots in 832 and the sepals in satin stitch using 245. Use stem stitch in 245 to work the stems and trailing vines. Stitch the dark leaves with fishbone stitch and the light leaves in open fishbone stitch. For the flowers and flower buds use flat stitch in 301. Finally, add the tiny flies with individual fly stitches using 832.

Flat Stitch

FLAT STITCH is a filling stitch that is worked like open fishbone stitch (page 44) but with a greater overlap in the centre and with the stitches closer together. It has a dense, slightly raised finish and can work very well when used to describe petals as in Strawberries page 45. Use additional guidelines to help you stitch accurately.

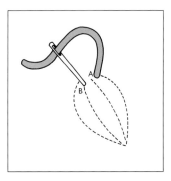

Fig 1. Bring the needle out at A and insert it at B on one of the centre guidelines.

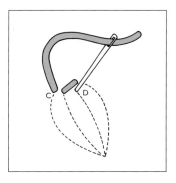

Fig 2. Bring the needle out at C on the other side of the shape and take it back down at D.

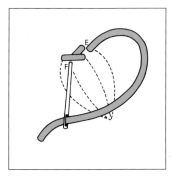

Fig 3. Bring the needle out at E and take it back down at F. Continue in the same way to complete the shape.

Fly Stitch

FLY STITCH is a versatile looped stitch that can be used singly or worked in rows as a border or filling. In the design on page 45 it is used individually to suggest tiny insects, but it is also excellent for filling leaves or for suggesting grasses.

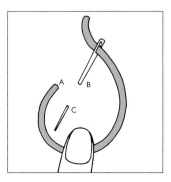

Fig 1. Bring the needle out at A and hold down the thread. Insert the needle a little to the right on the same level at B and bring it through at C, midway between A and B but lower down.

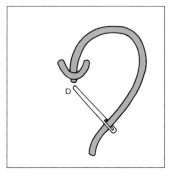

Fig 2. Keeping the thread under the needle, pull the thread through. Insert the needle at D to make a small tying stitch in the centre.

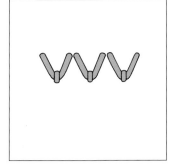

Fig 3. Fly stitches can be worked individually or in rows, either horizontally, as here, or vertically as in Fig 4. The length of the tying stitch can be short, as shown here, or lengthened so that the stitch resembles a 'Y' as in Dandelions on page 43.

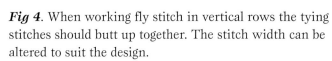

Fig 4. When working fly stitch in vertical rows the tying stitches should butt up together. The stitch width can be altered to suit the design.

French Knot

French knots create an effect like tiny beads, adding wonderful textural interest to a design. They can be worked singly, in a line or grouped together as a highly textured filling stitch. Use them singly for the spots of a butterfly as in the Lavender design on page 49, or group them for a flower centre as in the Floral Garland on page 37.

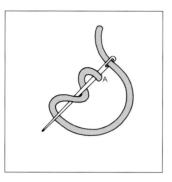

Fig 1. Bring the needle out at A, where the knot will be and wrap the thread once or twice around it.

Fig 2. Holding the thread firmly, twist the needle back round and insert it close to A.

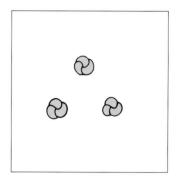

Fig 3. Holding the knot down, pull the thread through at the back and secure it with a small stitch (see page 14).

■ *Neat Results*

Avoid long threads running across the back of the work, which may show through in the finished piece. If French knots are worked in a block use the same thread for the next knot but when working them spaced apart tie off and start a new thread for each one.

Herringbone Stitch

Herringbone stitch has numerous uses: it can be worked in a row as a border, which can then be laced or threaded with contrasting threads, or massed in rows to make decorative bands for clothing or furnishings. It can also be used as a filling stitch as for the windows of the Christmas Cottage on page 31.

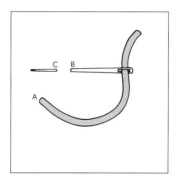

Fig 1. Bring the needle out at A on the lower design line. Insert it at B on the upper design line and bring it out at C.

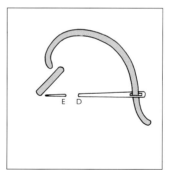

Fig 2. Insert the needle at D on the lower design line, bringing it out at E.

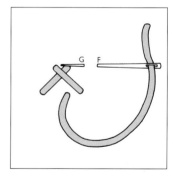

Fig 3. Insert the needle at F on the upper design line, bringing it out at G.

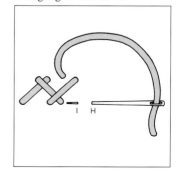

Fig 4. Insert the needle on the lower design line at H and bring it out at I. Continue in the same way to the end.

Closed Herringbone Stitch

CLOSED HERRINGBONE STITCH (double back stitch) is used for shadow work on fine, semi-transparent fabrics. It is used capture the translucency of the ribbon in the design shown opposite.

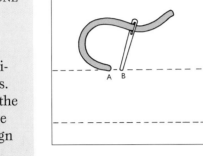

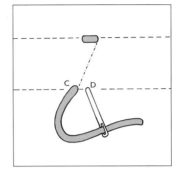

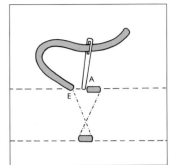

Fig 1. Bring the needle out at A and take a small back stitch, inserting it at B, as shown above.

Fig 2. Bring the needle out at C on the opposite side of the design area and insert it at D.

Fig 3. Bring the needle out at E and insert it at A.

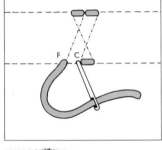

Fig 4. Bring the needle out at F and insert it at C. Continue in this way.

Leaf Stitch

LEAF STITCH is an open filling stitch with a woven central 'vein' that is ideal for leaf fillings, but it can also be used to fill shapes such as the lavender heads in the design opposite. Mark additional guidelines before you begin.

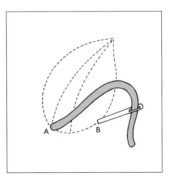

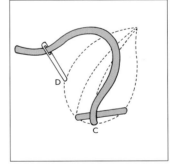

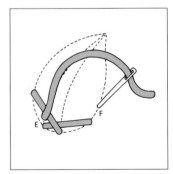

Fig 1. Bring the needle out at A and insert it at B to form a sloping stitch.

Fig 2. Bring the needle out at C and insert it at D.

Fig 3. Bring the needle out at E and insert it at F.

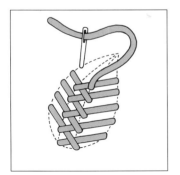

Fig 4. Continue the sequence, working stitches alternately on each side until the shape is filled and spacing stitches evenly, as shown.

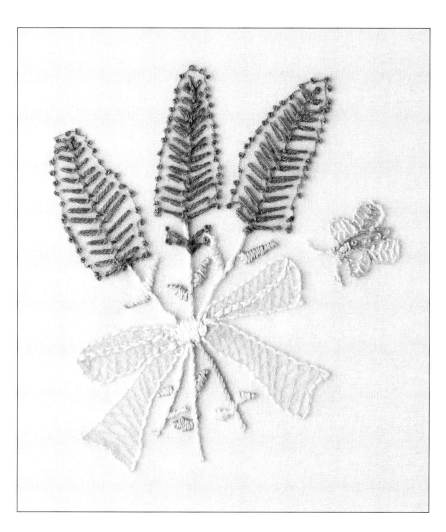

KEY
ANCHOR STRANDED
COTTON (FLOSS)

 110   1345 (multicolor)

291

FINISHED SIZE
10 x 9cm (4 x 3½in)

Stitching Notes

Lavender Bouquet

*This dainty design
is stitched on crystal
organza to allow the
shadow work of the bow
to show through. Use
water-soluble fabric
stabilizer to support the
fabric while stitching
and work with one
strand of thread unless
otherwise stated. Stitch
the lavender heads in leaf
stitch and then outline in
French knots all in 110,
deliberately trailing the
thread between each one
to achieve the effect. For
the stalks use stem stitch
with satin stitch for the
leaves, all in 1345. Using
the same thread, outline
the butterfly in stem stitch
and fill the wings with
leaf stitch and the body
with French knots. Now
work the bow in closed
herringbone stitch, using
two strands of 291.*

Long-and-Short Stitch

LONG-AND-SHORT STITCH is one of the most beautiful of all the filling stitches and an essential element of crewel embroidery. It looks like satin stitch, but the way it is worked enables you to create soft gradations of colour, as shown in the design opposite.

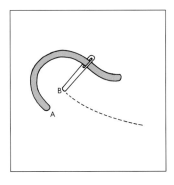

Fig 1. Bring the needle out at A and insert it at B.

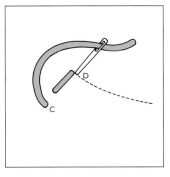

Fig 2. Bring the needle out at C and insert it at D, making a longer stitch that butts up tightly against the first stitch.

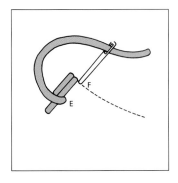

Fig 3. Make a stitch the same length as your first stitch, bringing the needle out at E and inserting it at F, as shown.

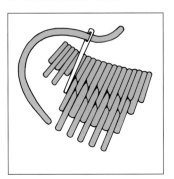

Fig 4. The stitches of subsequent rows should be the same length to maintain the zigzag pattern. Adjust the length of stitches on the final row to fit the design area.

Mountmellick Stitch

MOUNTMELLICK STITCH is a chunky outline stitch that was used for Mountmellick work, a type of whitework embroidery that originated in the town of Mountmellick in Ireland. Traditionally it was worked with matt cotton thread on white satin 'jean', but like all stitches it can be adapted to suit your purposes. It is used for the border in the Valentine Hearts design opposite.

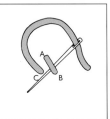

Fig 1. Bring the needle out at A, insert it at B and bring it out at C. Pull the thread through and then pass the needle under the stitch just made without piercing the fabric.

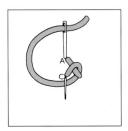

Fig 2. Pull the thread through and re-insert the needle at A, bringing it out at C and keeping the thread under the needle.

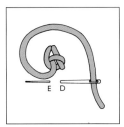

Fig 3. Pull the thread through. Insert the needle at D and bring it out to the left at E.

Fig 4. Pull the thread through then pass the needle under the last stitch, as shown.

Fig 5. Pull the thread through and re-insert the needle at C, bringing it out again at E with the thread under the needle. Continue in the same way.

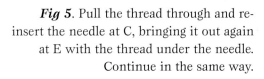

KEY

ANCHOR STRANDED
COTTON (FLOSS)

■	40		300
■	50	■	1201
■	216		

ANCHOR MARLITT

820

FINISHED SIZE

8 x 13cm (3 x 5⅛ in)

Stitching Notes

Valentine Hearts

Use two strands of thread to work this design. Start with the hearts, using long and short stitch and graduating from 40 at the bottom, through 1201 to 50 at the top. Outline each heart in running stitch in 40. Work the petals of the flowers in satin stitch using different shades of pink. Use 216 to work the stalks in stem stitch and the leaves in straight stitch. Add French knots in 300 at the centre of each flower and then add the yellow bow in satin stitch using 820. Add the two borders in Mountmellick stitch, using 216 for the inner border and 300 for the outer one.

■ Make it Personal

This design could be made into a lovely card or gift for a wedding or anniversary. Rather than filling the heart motifs with long-and-short stitch you could stitch the initials of the happy couple instead. Make sure you mark the letters on to the fabric before you stitch them so that you get a neat result.

Overcast Stitch

OVERCAST STITCH, also known as trailing stitch, is found in forms of whitework embroidery. It is a couching or laid-thread technique and is a useful outlining stitch, creating a neat raised line as featured on the urn in the design opposite.

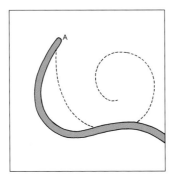

Fig 1. Bring the laid thread through at A.

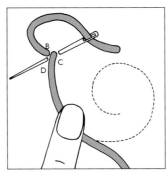

Fig 2. Hold the laid thread down and bring the working thread through at B. Insert the needle at C and bring it out at D.

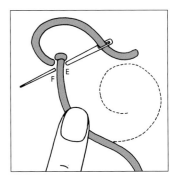

Fig 3. Pull the thread through. Insert the needle at E and bring it out at F, positioning this stitch close to the previous one. Continue making small stitches over the laid thread until you reach the end. Knot off both threads on the wrong side.

Raised Rose

RAISED ROSE is a little known stitch but quite easy to work and it is ideally suited for working rose flower forms as shown in the Topiary design opposite. It has small loops at the centre with loose stem stitch petals, giving it a raised, domed appearance.

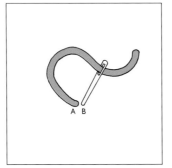

Fig 1. Bring the needle out at A and insert it at B, pulling the thread through to form a loop about 3mm (1/8in) high.

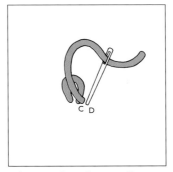

Fig 2. Bring the needle out at C and insert it at D to make a second loop.

Fig 3. Make two more loops and then work a small back stitch (page 24) at the base of the loops to secure the thread.

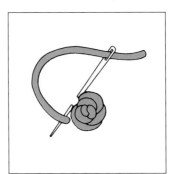

Fig 4. Work loose stem stitches (page 60) round the central cluster of loops to form 'petals', reducing the height of the rose towards the outer edge.

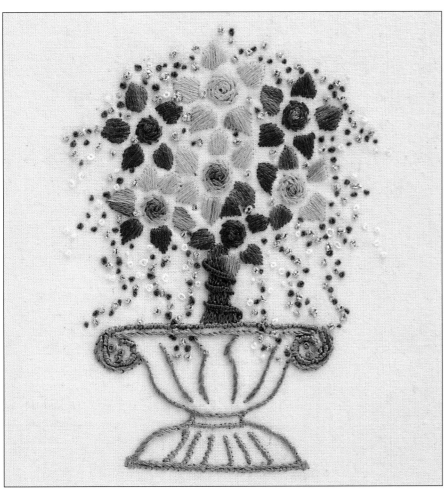

KEY

ANCHOR STRANDED
COTTON (FLOSS)

■	217	▨	1207

ANCHOR MARLITT

▨	1029	▨	1140
■	1039		

ANCHOR ARISTA 25 GRAM

▦	300

FINISHED SIZE
12 x 9cm (4¾ x 4½ in)

Stitching Notes

Topiary

Stitch this topiary design with two strands of thread unless otherwise stated. Work the top and bottom edges of the urn in overcast stitch and the rest of it in stem stitch using 1039. Work the stem of the standard rose in split stitch in 1140, using buttonhole stitch bar for the vine in 217. For the rose blooms use raised rose stitch in 1207 and for the loose petals use satin stitch. To create the effect of trailing leaves, work French knots around the roses in both greens, brown and gold Arista, using just one strand of the gold thread.

Raised Chain Band

RAISED CHAIN BAND produces a thick, raised effect when worked in close rows. It can be used for outlines or as a filling and is used in the design opposite for the stocking top band.

Fig 1. Work a row of closely spaced horizontal straight stitches to the required length for foundation bars. Bring the needle out at A and then, without piercing the fabric, pass the needle upwards under the first bar and to the left of A.

Fig 2. Now pass the needle under the bar to the right of A without piercing the fabric, keeping the thread under the needle. Pull through to form a loop.

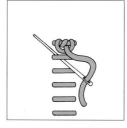

Fig 3. Insert the needle upwards to the left under the second bar, without piercing the fabric.

Fig 4. Insert the needle downwards under the same bar, keeping the thread under the needle. Continue until all the bars have been worked in this way.

Ribbed Wheel Filling

RIBBED WHEEL FILLING creates woven circles that add texture to a geometric design or can be used to suggest spiders' webs, snowflakes (as in the design opposite) or anything you decide.

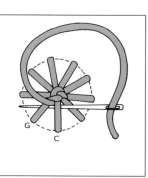

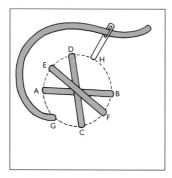

Fig 1. Bring the needle out at A and insert it across the circle but slightly off-centre at B. Work three more straight stitches, following the sequence C–D, E–F and G–H, as shown.

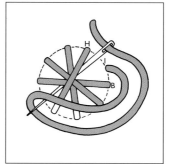

Fig 2. Bring the needle out at I. Using a tapestry needle, pass the needle under the four centre stitches without piercing the fabric. Wrap the thread over and under the needle.

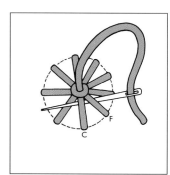

Fig 3. Pull the thread up to form a centre knot. Pass the needle under adjacent spokes F and C without piercing the fabric.

Fig 4. Pull the thread through and pass the needle back and under spokes C and G. Continue round the circle until the spokes are full and then fasten off at the back.

▥	150	☐	7001
▥	683	▥	7046

ANCHOR MARLITT

	845		1032
■	893		1078

FINISHED SIZE
12.5 x 12.5cm (5 x 5in)

 **Stitching Notes**

Christmas Stocking
Use one strand of pearl metallic thread and two strands of Marlitt to work this design. For the toe use 7001 to work scroll stitch. For the red area that follows use 893 in raised chain stitch. Work the instep in satin stitch using 1078 and the heel in 683, working rows of bokhara couching. Use 7046 to stitch the red area above the heel with detached buttonhole stitch and work the centre portion in satin stitch with 7001. Work the green area at the front with close rows of chain stitch in 1032 and stitch the blue area at the back with bokhara couching in 150. Stitch the band at the top in raised chain band using 1078 and 7001. Work the French knot swirls and ribbed wheel filling stars in 845.

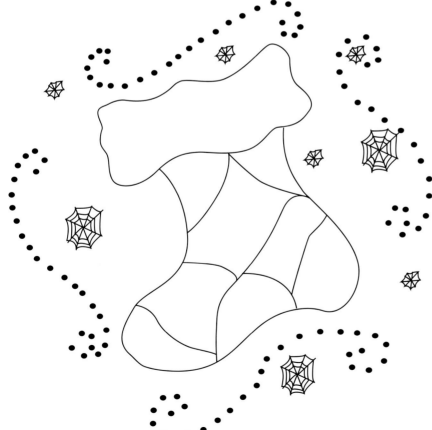

Rope Stitch

ROPE STITCH produces an attractive outline that, as its name suggests, looks rather like rope. It is ideal for capturing the texture of vines, trees, bulrushes and, of course, rope. In the Dandelions design on page 43 it is used to outline the leaves. It is a surprisingly simple stitch to work.

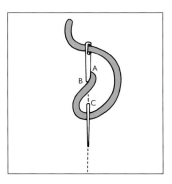

Fig 1. Bring the needle out at A, insert it at B and bring it back out at C on the design line, twisting the thread over and under the needle, as shown.

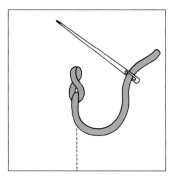

Fig 2. Set the stitch by pulling the thread downwards firmly to form a twisted loop.

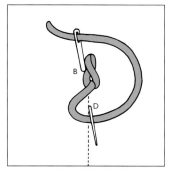

Fig 3. Insert the needle again at B in the curve of the first stitch, and bring it out at D with the thread under the needle as before. Continue in the same way, keeping the tension even.

Romanian Couching

ROMANIAN COUCHING, also called Romanian stitch, is a couching stitch that like Bokhara couching (page 26) uses just one thread for the laid work and the tying stitches. It can be worked to varying lengths to fill a shape. Its central vein makes it ideal for working leaves.

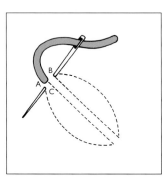

Fig 1. Bring the needle out at A, insert it at B and bring it out at C with the thread above the needle.

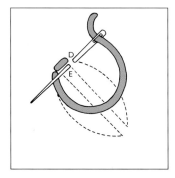

Fig 2. Insert the needle at D and bring it out at E on the first inner guideline with the thread under the needle, as shown.

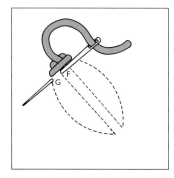

Fig 3. Insert the needle at F and bring it out at G.

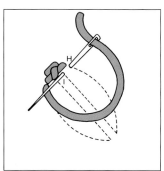

Fig 4. Insert the needle at H and bring it out at I with the thread under the needle. Continue in the same way.

Satin Stitch

SATIN STITCH is a filling stitch consisting entirely of straight stitches. Although it sounds easy, it takes practice to get the surface smooth and the edges even. It is an invaluable stitch and is used in many of the designs in this book including Nesting Ducks on page 63.

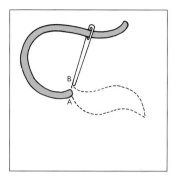

Fig 1. Bring the needle out at A and insert it at B.

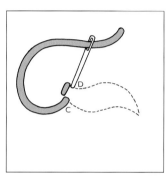

Fig 2. Bring the needle out at C and insert it at D. Continue in sequence, placing stitches close together so that no background fabric shows through and keeping the edges of the shape even and neat.

■ *Stitch Direction*
Satin stitches can be worked in different directions to catch the light and create areas of light and shade. When working many similar shapes, such as leaves, you may wish to work some at different angles, but do not work them at random or the result will look messy. With animals and birds it is best to follow the direction of fur or feathers.

Scroll Stitch

SCROLL STITCH is a knotted, wavy outline stitch that adds texture to a simple, linear design. It can also be used in conjunction with other stitches to make decorative bands. It is used for the Christmas Stocking on page 55 to suggest the knitted texture of the toe.

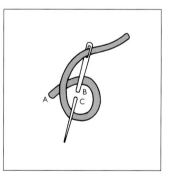

Fig 1. Bring the needle out at A and insert it at B, bringing it back out at C. Wrap the thread behind the needle and under the point and pull the needle through to form the stitch.

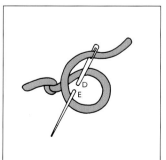

Fig 2. Insert the needle at D and bring it out at E, wrapping the thread behind the needle and under the point. Continue this sequence.

■ *Different Threads*
If you can't get the effect you are looking for, try changing to another thread. Scroll stitch produces a wide, flat line when worked in stranded cotton, but a raised effect in pearl cotton or coton à broder, for example.

Spider's Web Filling

SPIDER'S WEB FILLING produces a filled circle that can be used to depict flowers or simply round shapes in a geometric design. Unlike ribbed wheel filling (page 54), which has obvious spokes, this stitch has a close texture that makes it highly versatile. It features in Herbal Tea, shown opposite.

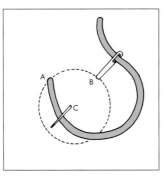

Fig 1. Bring the needle out at A and insert it at B. (A and B are one-fifth of the circumference apart.) Bring the needle through at C in the centre of the circle with the thread under the needle, as shown.

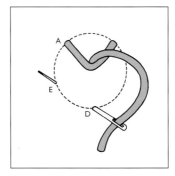

Fig 2. Insert the needle at D and bring it out at E, exactly between D and A.

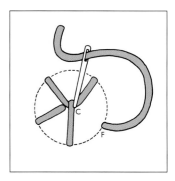

Fig 3. Insert the needle at the side of C and then bring it out at F. Insert it at the side of C again, bringing it back out beside C to secure the thread under the fabric.

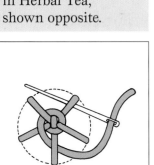

Fig 4. Use a tapestry needle (which has a rounded point) to weave the thread over and under the 'spokes' of the web until the circle is filled.

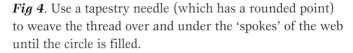

Split Stitch

SPLIT STITCH is a delicate outline stitch that, when worked correctly, looks like fine chain stitch. It can be worked in close rows as a filling stitch. It features on the flower petals in the design shown opposite.

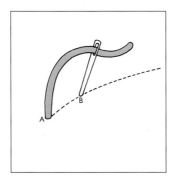

Fig 1. Bring the needle out at A and insert it at B.

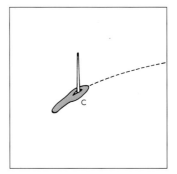

Fig 2. Bring the needle out at C, piercing the thread of the previous stitch.

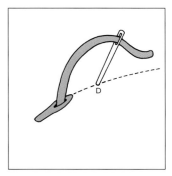

Fig 3. Insert the needle at D to form the next stitch and then bring the needle up to pierce the stitch just worked as before. Continue in this way.

KEY

FINISHED SIZE
10.5 x 11.5cm (4⅛ x 4½ in)

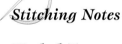

Stitching Notes

Herbal Tea

*Work this design with
two strands of embroidery
cotton unless otherwise
stated. Work the cup
outline with one strand of
130 in stem stitch. Work
the round flowers with
spider's web filling using
1077 and the other flowers
with split stitch using any
of your greens – I used
light green around the
edges with darker green in
the centre. Stitch a French
knot in the centre of these
flowers in your lighter
green. Work the stems
and trailing vines in stem
stitch and work the
leaves with 1215, using
cretan stitch.*

Stem Stitch

STEM STITCH is one of the most popular outlining stitches and the stitch most often chosen for working flower stems. To make the stitch wider, if required, simply increase the angle of each stitch. This stitch is used in Herbal Tea on page 59 to outline the cup and for the waves in the design opposite.

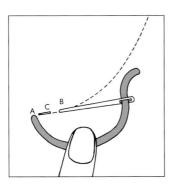

Fig 1. Bring the needle out at the start of the design line at A. Insert the needle at B and bring it out at C, midway between A and B, holding the thread to one side, as shown.

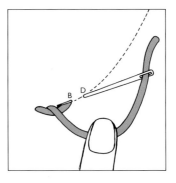

Fig 2. Pull the thread through to set the first stitch. Hold the working thread down with the thumb and insert the needle at D, bringing it back out at B.

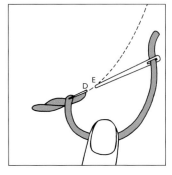

Fig 3. Insert the needle at E and bring it out at D. Continue in this way, making each stitch exactly the same length.

Straight Stitch

STRAIGHT STITCH is the simplest of all freestyle stitches and has a variety of applications and uses. In the diagrams stitches are shown worked in a daisy formation, but they can be worked in any formation or angle and singly, touching, overlapping or parallel. In All at Sea, opposite, it is used on the lighthouse.

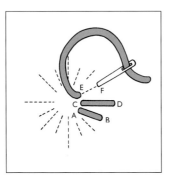

Fig 1. Work a single stitch over each design line. For this design work the straight stitches in the same way as satin stitch (page 57), bringing the needle out and A, C and E.

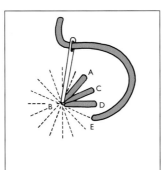

Fig 2. Straight stitches can share one or more hole(s). Here the stitches radiate out from a central point and are all the same length. Finish on the wrong side of the work with a small back stitch (page 24).

■ ***Random Effects***
Most embroidery stitches rely on a neat repetition of a stitch pattern. With straight stitch you can break the mould and create a change of pace by working stitches within a design area at random, overlapping at different angles and using several colours, if desired. This works particularly well for rendering wild grasses or dense undergrowth.

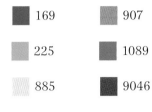

Stitching Notes

All at Sea

Stitch the waves in stem stitch using two strands. Use the same stitch with one strand to outline the sails (1009), hull (1089) and base of the cliffs (885). Work the mast and boom in soft cotton. Fill the sails, flag, cliffs and most of the lighthouse in satin stitch. Use split stitch with two strands to work the stripes on the lighthouse and hull and for the grass. Use stem stitch for the detail on the lighthouse and for the ropes and back stitch for the door. Work the birds in fly stitch. Add a French knot to the light, door and hull. Work the splashes with chain stitches.

Vandyke Stitch

VANDYKE STITCH is an attractive filling stitch, often used for leaf shapes because of its central 'vein', although it can also be used for a decorative border when worked to a fairly narrow, even width as shown here. In the design opposite it is used to delineate the wings in black.

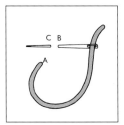

Fig 1. Bring the needle out at A on the left-hand edge and take a small stitch from B to C at the top of the design area.

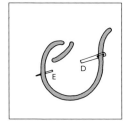

Fig 2. Pull the thread taut, insert the needle at D (on the same level as A) and bring it back out at E.

Fig 3. Without piercing the fabric, pass the needle under the crossed threads, as shown.

Fig 4. Pull the thread taut, insert the needle at F (on the same level as E), and bring it back out at G.

Fig 5. Repeat the sequence, passing the needle under the crossed threads immediately above until the shape is filled or the border finished.

Wheatear Stitch

WHEATEAR STITCH is a looped stitch that looks like an ear of wheat. It can be used for borders or plant forms and can have a special place in geometrical designs. It is best in straight rows or gentle curves. It is used in the design opposite for the nest. You may find it helpful to draw in additional guidelines.

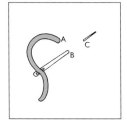

Fig 1. Bring the needle out at A. Insert it at B, bringing it back out at C.

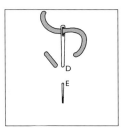

Fig 2. Insert the needle at D and bring it out at E.

Fig 3. Without piercing the fabric, pass the needle under the two straight stitches.

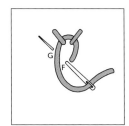

Fig 4. Insert the needle at F and bring it out at G to complete one stitch.

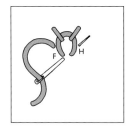

Fig 5. Insert the needle at F and bring it out at H. Continue working in sequence.

KEY

ANCHOR STRANDED
COTTON (FLOSS)

| | 227 | | 403 |
| | 823 | | 9046 |

ANCHOR MARLITT

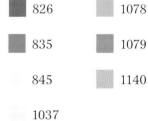

	826		1078
	835		1079
	845		1140
	1037		

FINISHED SIZE
9.5 x 13cm (3¾ x 5⅛in)

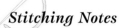

Stitching Notes

Ducks

Stitch the heads of the ducks in satin stitch using one strand of 227 for the drake and two strands of 823 for the duck. Use the same stitch for the main part of their feathers, beaks (1078), the drake's feet (1079) and reed heads. Outline the drake's feet with split stitch. Use straight stitch for the tail feathers, neck bands, plant and reed stalks. Work the black bands on the feathers in Vandyke stitch and use the same stitch for the bank. Work the nest in wheatear stitch, then use stem stitch for the stripes on the ducks and for the lines in the water. Add the flowers and eyes with French knots.

Suppliers

UK
Coats Crafts UK
PO Box 22, Lingfield House, Lingfield Point, McMullen
Road, Darlington Co. Durham DL1 1YQ
Tel: + 1 325 394237 (Consumer Helpline)
Fax: + 1 325 394200
www.coatscrafts.co.uk

USA
Coats and Clark
PO Box 12229
Greenville
SC 29612-0229
Tel: (800) 648 1479
www.coatsandclark.com

Index

bag 16–19, 37
bars, buttonhole 28
borders 26, 36, 38, 40, 46, 47, 50, 62

designs
    All at Sea 61
    Butterflies 35
    Celebration Cake 25
    Christmas
        Cottage 31
        Stocking 55, 57
    Dandelion 20, 43, 46, 56
    Floral Garland 16–19, 37
    Herbal Tea 59
    Japanese Lady 27
    Lavender Sachet 21, 48, 49
    Nesting Ducks 63
    Poppies 15, 33
    Strawberries 45
    Topiary 6, 52, 53
    Underwater Garden 41
    Valentine Hearts 51

edgings 24, 28–9
equipment 6, 7–9

fabric 7, 18
filling stitches 26, 30, 32, 34, 38, 39, 40, 42, 44, 46, 47, 48, 50, 54, 57, 58, 62
finishing work 14
flowers 6, 16, 20–1, 26, 33, 37, 45, 49, 52, 53, 58–9, 60, 62
frames/framing 7–8, 12–13, 22–3

greetings cards 51
guidelines 15

hoops 7–8, 12

knots 14, 24, 26, 29, 32, 40, 42, 47

lacing your work 23
leaves 37, 39, 42, 44–5, 46, 48, 56, 62

materials 7–9

needles 8

outlining 24, 26, 30, 32, 34, 36, 40, 42, 50, 52, 54, 56, 57, 58, 60

scissors 9
shadow work 48, 49
snowflakes 54, 55
spider's web 54, 58
starting work 14
stitches
    Antwerp edging 24
    back stitch 24, 48
    Bokhara couching 26
    bullion 14, 26
    buttonhole 28–9
    cable 30, 32
    chain 30, 31, 32, 33, 34, 36, 58
    chevron 38
    couching 26, 38, 39, 52, 56
    Cretan 39
    double knot 40

feather stitch 15, 36, 40, 42
fern 42
fishbone 15, 44
flat 15, 46
fly 43, 46
French knot 14, 47
herringbone 47–8
Jacobean couching 39
leaf 15, 48
long-and-short 50
Mountmellick 50
overcast 52
raised chain band 54
raised rose 52
ribbed wheel filling 54
Romanian couching 56
rope 56
satin 57
scroll 57
Spanish knotted feather 42
spider's web filling 58
split 58
stem 60
straight 60
Vandyke 62
wheatear 62

tacking 11
tension 12, 14–15
texture 26, 28, 40, 44, 47, 54, 56, 57, 58
thread 9, 14, 57
towel band 20, 43
transferring a design 10–11, 15